This edition published by Parragon Books Ltd in 2017

Parragon Books Ltd
Chartist House
15–17 Trim Street
Bath BA1 1HA, UK
www.parragon.com

Copyright © Parragon Books Ltd 2017

Illustrated by: Dubravka Kolanovic
Reading consultant: Geraldine Taylor

All rights reserved. No part of this publication may be reproduced, stored in a retrieval system or transmitted, in any form or by any means, electronic, mechanical, photocopying, recording or otherwise, without the prior permission of the copyright holder.

ISBN 978-1-4748-6307-0

Printed in China

FIRST READERS
Little Red Riding Hood

PaRragon
Bath • New York • Cologne • Melbourne • Delhi
Hong Kong • Shenzhen • Singapore

Five steps for enjoyable reading

Traditional stories and fairy tales are a great way to begin reading practice. The stories and characters are familiar and lively. Follow the steps below to help your child become a confident and independent reader.

Step 1
Read the story aloud to your child. Run your finger under the words as you read.

Step 2
Look at the pictures and talk about what is happening.

Step 3
Read the simple text on the right-hand page together. When reading, some words come up again and again, such as **the**, **to** or **and**. Your child will quickly learn to recognize these high-frequency words by sight.

ittle Red Riding Hood set off
see Granny.

Step 4
When your child is ready, encourage them to read the simple lines on their own.

Step 5
Help your child to complete the puzzles at the back of the book.

In a faraway wood, there lived a kind girl called Little Red Riding Hood. She was taking a basket of food to her sick granny.

"Remember to go straight to Granny's house," said Little Red Riding Hood's mother. "Don't stray off the path and don't talk to any strangers!"

Little Red Riding Hood set off to see Granny.

Little Red Riding Hood followed the path through the woods. She hummed a little tune as she swung her basket. She saw lots of pretty blue flowers. But she didn't see the wolf hiding in the trees!

"Hello, little girl," said the big bad wolf. "What are you doing?"

Little Red Riding Hood jumped with fright. "I'm going to see my sick granny, who lives in the little house in the woods," she said.

"What a kind girl you are," said the wolf. "I'm sure your granny will like these pretty blue flowers. Why don't you stay and pick some for her?"

He smiled, showing his big white teeth.

The big bad wolf
ran off into the woods.

While Little Red Riding Hood stayed to pick some blue flowers, the big bad wolf ran all the way to Granny's house...and gobbled her up! He put on Granny's cap and glasses.

The big bad wolf got into Granny's bed.

Soon afterwards, Little Red Riding Hood arrived at Granny's house.
The door was wide open. Little Red Riding Hood walked in.

"Are you in bed, Granny?" she called.

Little Red Riding Hood went into the bedroom. She walked up to the bed. Granny didn't look very well!

"Oh, Granny!" Little Red Riding Hood said. "What big ears you have!"

"All the better to hear you with, my dear," said the wolf in a granny voice.

Granny had very big ears!

"Oh, Granny!" said Little Red Riding Hood. "What big eyes you have!"

"All the better to see you with, my dear," said the wolf in his granny voice.

Little Red Riding Hood thought Granny looked odd.

"Oh, Granny!" said Little Red Riding Hood. "What big teeth you have!"

"All the better to eat you with!" growled the wolf. He opened his mouth wide and leaped at Little Red Riding Hood.

The big bad wolf ate Little Red Riding Hood!

Luckily, a woodcutter was passing Granny's cottage. He went inside to visit Granny and found the big bad wolf taking a nap.

The woodcutter turned the wolf upside down and gave him a good shake.

Out came Granny and Little Red Riding Hood!

Granny, Little Red Riding Hood and the woodcutter all chased the big bad wolf.
The big bad wolf ran away.

And they never saw him again.

Puzzle time!

Which two words rhyme?

see   bed   red   bad   big

Which word does not match
the picture?

ear
eyes
axe

Which word matches the picture?

good
wood
hood

Who had the basket?

Little Red Riding Hood
Granny
Woodcutter

Which sentence is right?

The big bad wolf ran away.
The big bad wolf ran back.

Answers
Which two words rhyme? **bed** and **red**
Which word does not match the picture? **axe**
Which word matches the picture? **wood**
Who had a basket? **Little Red Riding Hood**
Which sentence is right? **The big bad wolf ran away.**